GOD'S LITTLE BOOK OF LIFE

HarperCollins*Publishers*
1 London Bridge Street
London SE1 9GF

www.harpercollins.co.uk

HarperCollins*Publishers*
1st Floor, Watermarque Building, Ringsend Road
Dublin 4, Ireland

First published by HarperCollins*Publishers* in 2021

1 3 5 7 9 10 8 6 4 2

Copyright © HarperCollins*Publishers* 1998, 2017, 2020, 2021

Richard Daly asserts the moral right to be identified as the author of this work

A catalogue record for this book is available from the British Library

ISBN 978-0-00-850032-0

Printed and bound in Latvia

MIX
Paper from
responsible sources
FSC™ C007454

This book is produced from independently certified FSC™ paper
to ensure responsible forest management.

For more information visit: www.harpercollins.co.uk/green

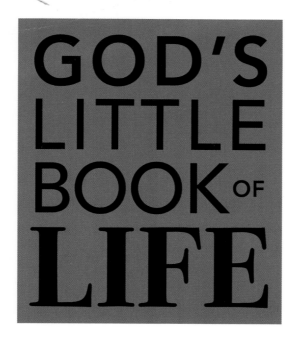

GOD'S LITTLE BOOK OF LIFE

RICHARD DALY

WILLIAM
COLLINS

Peace

WORDS OF COMFORT
AND REASSURANCE

INTRODUCTION

In a world where distress and anxiety have become the norms, how can we truly experience peace in a peaceless world?

Harmony amongst nations and between people struck by terror and disaster is hard to come by. Yet in the midst of turmoil, peace can still be achieved. It is possible to live in a world without peace, and yet still be in peace. Such an experience comes only from knowing God.

This chapter is designed to provide you with insightful words to help you discover true peace for yourself.

KNOW GOD, KNOW PEACE ...
NO GOD, NO PEACE

One of the many titles given to God is
"Jehovah-Shalom," which means "the God of
Peace." Our first step in finding true peace
is getting to know God.

For Further Reflection

Judges 6:24

WISH PEACE

The Jewish word for peace is "shalom."
Its meaning signifies a deep inner wellbeing
that is often wished upon someone in
greeting. Greet someone today in this
way and wish peace into their life.

For Further Reflection

Daniel 4:1

GET CONNECTED

The greatest quest in life has always been
the search for peace. Many have traveled
far and wide, yet the path to peace is a direct
line between God and man … the oneness
of divinity and humanity.

For Further Reflection

Jeremiah 29:13

THINK TRANQUILITY

Tranquillity—what a peaceful word.
Picture yourself in a tranquil scene—
by a calm flowing river, a serene sunset,
a quiet meadow. This in itself aids
peace of mind.

For Further Reflection

Philippians 4:7

SEEK A PEACEFUL REMEDY

It's not work that wears us out, but
worry, anxiety, stress, fear, and everything
else that perplexes our minds. Inner peace
is the only antidote that banishes these
negative emotions.

For Further Reflection

Colossians 3:15

PURSUE PEACE

Worry is something you permit; peace
is something you pursue. That means
you can learn to control what goes on
in your mind.

For Further Reflection

John 14:7

THINK PEACEFUL THOUGHTS

Agitation! Frustration! Complication! Just
the thought of these gives a sense of unrest.
Calm, tranquillity, serenity ... now doesn't
that just feel better?

For Further Reflection

Philippians 4:8

CLEAR YOUR CONSCIENCE

What greater peace of mind can be
achieved than when you know you are
doing God's will?

For Further Reflection

Isaiah 48:18
Ephesians 5:17

GOD IS BIG!

To worry is to say to God, "You're not big enough to solve this problem, so I'll deal with it myself." Remember, you don't have a problem he can't solve.

For Further Reflection

Psalm 24:8
Psalm 121

KNOW YOUR LIMITS

Peace disappears when you try to do something about something you can't do anything about!

For Further Reflection

Matthew 19:26
Genesis 18:14

DELEGATE YOUR WORRIES

Ninety-two percent of what we worry
about, we have no control over. Give the
other eight percent to God and bask
in peace of mind.

For Further Reflection

Psalm 55:22
1 Peter 5:7

KILL OVERWORK, NOT YOURSELF

If you make your work more important
than yourself, you won't be around to
finish it.

For Further Reflection

Matthew 11:28–30
Romans 14:17

LIVE PEACE

"Let peace rule": that ought to
be your motto!

For Further Reflection

Colossians 3:15
Isaiah 55:12

TAKE A BREAK

Never feel guilty about taking a break—
God didn't. Time taken in rest replenishes
your soul and aids a peaceful spirit.

For Further Reflection

Hebrews 4:3–5

EXPERIENCE HEAVEN IN HELL

When all hell is breaking loose around you,
yet you remain calm and confident, you're
experiencing the peace of God that
transcends all understanding.

For Further Reflection

Philippians 4:7

JUST PRAY

Inner peace need not be all that elusive.
Just pray for it.

For Further Reflection

Philippians 4:6–7
Jeremiah 29:7

CHANGE YOUR MIND

Don't waste time focusing on things you can't change. Instead focus on things you can, like your perspective and attitude toward life.

For Further Reflection

Isaiah 26:3

LIVE FOR TODAY

Live one peaceful day at a time. Remember, yesterday is gone and tomorrow is unborn; all you have is today.

For Further Reflection

Matthew 6:25
Matthew 6:11

LOOK TO THIS DAY

Today well lived makes every yesterday
a dream of happiness and every tomorrow
a vision of hope.

For Further Reflection

Psalm 118:24
2 Corinthians 6:2

WORK THROUGH YOUR PROBLEMS

Whatever problem is destroying your
peace, ask: What is the worst that can
possibly happen? Then prepare to accept
it, and peacefully proceed to improve
on the worst.

For Further Reflection

Romans 8:28, 31

FEAR NOT

Fear is the opposite of peace.

For Further Reflection

1 John 4:18

BE REJUVENATED

Peacefulness promotes the most relaxing
recreating forces—good health, good sleep,
laughter, and happiness.

For Further Reflection

Isaiah 58:8

SEEK WISDOM IN PROVERBS

"Don't cross your bridges before you come
to them" and "don't cry over spilt milk" are two
old proverbs that can lead to a peaceful life.

For Further Reflection

Romans 12:16

THINK PEACE, GAIN PEACE

Think miserable thoughts and be miserable.
Think fearful thoughts and be fearful.
Think peaceful thoughts and be peaceful.
You are what you think!

For Further Reflection

2 Corinthians 10:5
Proverbs 23:7

DON'T HOLD GRUDGES

To forgive is a powerful release of
pent-up feelings. It leads to freedom.
Freedom leads to peace.

For Further Reflection

2 Corinthians 2:7
Romans 12:17

BE GRATEFUL

Be grateful for what you have. A spirit
of appreciation goes a long way to
peaceful feelings.

For Further Reflection

Ephesians 5:20
Job 1:21
Hebrews 13:5

COUNT YOUR BLESSINGS

It's not until something is taken away from
you that you realize its importance. Count
your blessings, not your troubles.

For Further Reflection

Ephesians 1:3
Hebrews 13:5

TURN YOUR MINUS TO PLUS

One of the traits of having a peaceful
character is the ability to turn unpleasant
experiences into positive lessons. Start
doing that today.

For Further Reflection

Jeremiah 31:13
Psalm 30:5

BE INTERESTED IN OTHERS

In whatever problem you experience, there's
always someone worse off than you. Discover
other people's plights; it may make yours
pale into insignificance.

For Further Reflection

Psalm 41:1
Proverbs 14:21
Galatians 6:2

SPREAD PEACE

Peace is contagious. Live peacefully and
it will rub off on people around you.

For Further Reflection

Isaiah 52:7–9

SEEK RECONCILIATION

When you are at peace with others, you will
ultimately be at peace with yourself.

For Further Reflection

Hebrews 12:14
Matthew 5:23–24

TELL GOD EVERYTHING!

"Oh what peace we often forfeit,
Oh what needless pain we bear
All because we do not carry
Everything to God in prayer."

For Further Reflection

Matthew 7:7–8
John 14:13–14

UNBURDEN YOUR HEART

Any psychiatrist will tell you it is
therapeutic to share your problems. If you
can't tell anyone trustworthy, you can
always trust God.

For Further Reflection

Jeremiah 33:3
Isaiah 59:1

REPRODUCE PEACE

Peace begets peace. Each day ask
God to help you become an instrument
of his peace.

For Further Reflection

Nahum 1:15

BE STILL

The very word peace emits a sense of stillness. Just being still long enough will give you a vision of what peace can be.

For Further Reflection

Psalm 46:10

BE OF ONE MIND

Worry comes from the Greek word meaning to "divide the mind." Peace counteracts that and restores your mind to oneness.

For Further Reflection

Philippians 4:2
Luke 12:29–31

SPEAK TRUTHFULLY

Honesty is still the best policy and leads
to inner contentment. Deception, falsity,
and even half-truths will stifle your
search for peace.

For Further Reflection

John 8:32
Philippians 4:8

RELAX

It has been clinically proven that any
nervous or emotional state fails to exist in
the presence of complete relaxation.
Make time to relax today.

For Further Reflection

Psalm 37:7–11

TAKE A POWER NAP

Rest is not doing "nothing." Rest is repair.
A five-minute nap during the day will
help restore peaceful vitalities.

For Further Reflection
Mark 6:31–32

HOPE

There are many people living with no hope.
Hope gives you purpose and direction;
it is the oil that fuels peace.

For Further Reflection
Romans 15:13

SEEK FORGIVENESS

Ultimate peace begins when we have
peace with God. Regardless of your past,
he is willing to forgive and forget.
Just ask him.

For Further Reflection

Romans 5:1
1 John 1:9

APPRECIATE YOURSELF

Peace is also dependent on how we feel
about ourselves. A routine of exercise
generates a feel-good factor.

For Further Reflection

Ephesians 5:29

EAT HEALTHILY

Are you eating properly? If you aren't,
it will affect your energy levels, your
moods, and hence your peace.

For Further Reflection

1 Corinthians 6:19–20
Ephesians 5:29

PACE YOURSELF

Stress wears down your immune system
and makes you vulnerable to the very
things you fear.

For Further Reflection

Proverbs 19:2

TRUST IN GOD

Trust is the highest form of faith because
it doesn't need to know all the answers …
trust God and let peace take over.

For Further Reflection

Proverbs 3:5–6
2 Samuel 22:3

BE CONTENT

It is better to be content with little than
anxious having too much. Peace is not about
what or who you are, but how you are.

For Further Reflection

Luke 3:14

JUST SAY NO

The demands of life can be overwhelming.
In order for peace to flourish, learn to say "no."

For Further Reflection

Galatians 5:22–23

ACCEPT HIS LOVE

No matter how unworthy you feel today,
nothing can shut off God's flowing
love for you.

For Further Reflection

Songs of Solomon 8:7
John 3:16

BELIEVE GOD!

God's opinion of you, and his opinion alone,
is the only reliable basis on which to build
your self-worth. Never forget that!

For Further Reflection
Isaiah 43:1–2
Psalm 139:1–24

RELAX YOUR MUSCLES

Right now, unless your entire body is as limp
as an old rag doll, you are at this very
moment producing nervous and muscular
tensions. Relax, relax, relax.

For Further Reflection
Psalm 46:10

MAKE PEACE A HABIT

Tension is a habit. Relaxing is a habit.
Bad habits can be broken, good habits
can be developed.

For Further Reflection

Ephesians 5:15

AVOID A "MUST DO" ATTITUDE

What limits peace? A sense of "must" or
"obligation"; the unending list of things ahead
that simply have to be done!

For Further Reflection

Ecclesiastes 3:1–9

READ PSALM 23

Psalm 23 provides a wonderful picture of tranquillity and peace: "He leads me to lie down in green pastures, he leads me beside still waters, he restores my soul".

For Further Reflection
Psalm 23

LET OTHERS JUDGE

You will instinctively know if you are in a state of peacefulness and those around you will know, too … including your dog!

For Further Reflection
Matthew 5:16

LET GOD HEAL

Broken relationships can often lead to
broken hearts. God promises to heal the
broken-hearted. Not only does he heal,
he also restores.

For Further Reflection

Psalm 147:3
Psalm 145:14–15
Jeremiah 30:17

FORGIVE OTHERS

Forgiving others not only releases you,
it frees the offender. Both of you can
then move on in life.

For Further Reflection

Mark 9:50

MAKE PEACEFUL CHOICES

Major decisions in life often cause anxiety.
Avoid it by taking time to pray and seek
godly counsel before you proceed.

For Further Reflection
Jeremiah 29:11–13

BE A MEDIATOR

Mediation involves being a "go-between"
for two people in need. It is the ultimate
way to become a peacemaker.

For Further Reflection
Matthew 5:9
Ephesians 4:2–4

EMBRACE GOD'S PEACE

World peace is very much an illusion.
But with the peace of God, you can live
peacefully in a peaceless world.

For Further Reflection

John 14:27

GO SOMEWHERE PEACEFUL

To evoke peace go to a place of peace:
a quiet garden; beside a babbling brook—any
place where your soul can be uplifted.

For Further Reflection

Isaiah 32:18
1 Timothy 2:2

WISH PEACE TO OTHERS

Keep praying for peace in war-torn countries.
Your prayers could be their only hope.

For Further Reflection

Luke 10:5

SPIRITUALITY LEADS TO PEACE

The Bible counsels that to have our minds
"on the world" leads to death, but to be
spiritually-minded leads to peace and life.

For Further Reflection

Romans 8:6

SLOW DOWN

The tempo of modern life is not conducive
to rest and relaxation. Slow down! There's
no one winner in the race of life.

For Further Reflection
1 Corinthians 9:24–27

STAY STRONG

When you're at your lowest point and
everything you've tried has failed, don't
throw in the towel—you may be closer to
a breakthrough than you think!

For Further Reflection
Isaiah 54:17

ACTUALIZE

Talk peaceful to be peaceful.

For Further Reflection

Colossians 4:6

LEAVE IT TO GOD

What you can't accomplish by worrying
all night, God can accomplish in an instant
by his spoken word.

For Further Reflection

Psalm 46:6–7

LIVE PEACEABLY

There is calmness when life is lived
in gratitude and quiet joy.

For Further Reflection

Psalm 107:29–30

SPEAK PEACEFULLY

Your words are like nitro-glycerine: they
can either blow up bridges or heal hearts.
Be careful what you say; in your tongue
lays the power of life or death.

For Further Reflection

Romans 12:18
Isaiah 50:4–7

DON'T LOSE YOUR PEACE

Next time you get all worked up, ask yourself:
What is the enemy trying to do?
His plan is to steal your joy.

For Further Reflection

Exodus 14:14
Job 13:5

CONTROL YOUR THOUGHTS

Direct your thoughts to those virtues
that inspire you—hope, joy, love,
and thankfulness.

For Further Reflection

Jeremiah 29:11
Luke 24:38–39

BITTER TO SWEETNESS

Betrayal is something others do to you.
Bitterness is something you develop yourself!
Look past the hurt and you'll see that
your resentment is just a roadblock to
your own peace.

For Further Reflection

Ephesians 4:31
Hebrews 12:15

GUARD YOUR MIND!

We are encouraged to "take captive every
thought and make it obedient to Christ."
When we actively police our minds, our
defence will begin to grow strong.

For Further Reflection

2 Corinthians 5:10

BE AT PEACE WITH YOURSELF

When you withhold forgiveness you hurt
yourself more—much more! It hangs
over you like a cloud, affecting everything
you do. Forgiveness releases peace and
restoration. So forgive today!

For Further Reflection
Matthew 6:12
1 Kings 8:50

LOVE IN ACTION

All genuine works of love are works
of peace. So keep loving.

For Further Reflection
Matthew 5:44
Luke 6:35

BE HONEST

If you always tell the truth, you never have
to worry about remembering what you said.
Nothing is more important than credibility.
Lose that and you can lose everything.

For Further Reflection

Romans 12:17

SMILE AWHILE

Peace starts with a smile. It's as
simple as that!

For Further Reflection

Numbers 6:26

ENCOURAGE SOMEONE TODAY

One basic human need is to be appreciated.
We all think wonderful things about people
but never tell them. Praise becomes valuable
only when you impart it. Tell someone today
how much you appreciate them.

For Further Reflection

Romans 12:6–8

PEACE BEGETS PEACE

The peace of God enables us to live in
peace with God, with ourselves, and with
our fellow man.

For Further Reflection

Romans 5:1

JUST LISTEN

One word from God—just one word—
can change everything for you. Take time
out to listen for that word today.

For Further Reflection

Ezekiel 4:7
2 Kings 20:16

LET GOD LEAD

When you surrender to Christ, you look
at life through his eyes. This enables you
to handle life through his strength.

For Further Reflection

John 14:16

SLEEP WELL!

Sleep is a gift from God. The Psalmist says:
It is vain to sit up late … for so he gives up
his beloved sleep. Maybe the most spiritual
thing you can do right now is put this
book down and take a nap!

For Further Reflection

Psalm 127:2
Ecclesiastes 5:12

LOVE ONE ANOTHER

Anything that makes it difficult to love our
fellow man makes it difficult to love God.

For Further Reflection

John 13:34
1 John 4:7

DON'T LEAVE OUT GOD

Don't get so involved in the work of God
that you neglect the God of the work!

For Further Reflection

John 15:5

A COMFORT THOUGHT

The Holy Spirit is our comforter.
Isn't that comforting to know?

For Further Reflection

John 14:16
John 14:26

PRAY

When in need, pray this prayer:
Prince of peace I need you. Take charge.
I need comfort and courage that comes
from your Spirit. Let me find you in a quiet
place where I can hear your heartbeat
and feel secure. Amen.

For Further Reflection
Psalm 62:8

LET PEACE FLOW

When the Holy Spirit fills your life,
you immediately become a channel
of God's love and his peace.

For Further Reflection
Psalm 37:11

CONTROL YOURSELF

"Self" will always find reasons to be
dissatisfied. Your spirit will always search for
reasons to be thankful. Both are in conflict;
the winner depends on you.
Let your spirit rule.

For Further Reflection

1 Thessalonians 5:18

LEARN FROM OTHERS

Read the scriptures and see how often
the peace of God sustained and carried
people through, even Jesus Christ.

For Further Reflection

John 5:39

TRUST IN GOD

By maintaining your peace when under attack, you're telling the Devil, "I'm still trusting in God." This baffles the enemy.

For Further Reflection
Ephesians 6:13

SEEK RECONCILIATION

Jesus said: When you offer your gift at the altar, and you remember that someone has something against you, leave your gift and go and make peace first. It's still the best advice for reconciliation.

For Further Reflection
Matthew 5:23–24

AMAZING GRACE

Never underestimate the glorious gift of grace. Jesus gave his life for you and wishes to grant you complete restoration.

For Further Reflection

Ephesians 2:8

PERFECT LOVE

Whatever your circumstances, always remember that God loves you with an unfathomable love that cannot be measured, and that is totally perfect.

For Further Reflection

Jeremiah 31:3
Nahum 1:7

HE THAT IS GREATER

Remember there is One greater than you,
in whom all fear dissolves.

For Further Reflection

1 John 4:4

GAIN EVERLASTING PEACE

Jesus is the same yesterday, today,
and forever. This means the peace he
offers is timeless.

For Further Reflection

Hebrews 13:8

CLAIM GOD'S GIFT
Peace is the gift of God.

For Further Reflection
1 John 4:18
2 Timothy 1:7

AVOID DOUBT
It will surprise you how often the thing you
fear the most will never come to pass.

For Further Reflection
Deuteronomy 1:21
Matthew 21:21

GRATITUDE

Having a spirit of gratitude is like a tonic:
it smoothes the ruffled brow and places a
smile upon the countenance.

For Further Reflection

1 Samuel 12:24
Psalm 126:3

MULTIPLY YOUR BLESSINGS

There are two ways to multiply our blessings.
One is to recognize them, the other is to
share them.

For Further Reflection

Ephesians 1:3

REST

The way of escape that God offers us is not a flight, but a release. He says: "Come unto me and I will give you rest."

For Further Reflection

Matthew 11:28
Exodus 20:8–11

BE FREE IN CHRIST

When you know your sins are truly forgiven, you know you are truly free.

For Further Reflection

Galatians 5:1

LEAVE IT WITH GOD

Having turned your problem over to God,
cease worrying and go peacefully about
other duties. It is no longer your matter,
but his.

For Further Reflection

Psalm 55:22

THE FUTURE IS BRIGHT WITH GOD

Worry is blind and cannot discern the future,
but God sees the end from the beginning.

For Further Reflection

Revelation 1:8

SPREAD LOVE

If feeling despondent, visit someone not as fortunate as you. Pass on a cheery word of comfort. I guarantee you will feel lifted too.

For Further Reflection
Galatians 6:2

USE YOUR IMAGINATION

We are told worry is what continues after a danger is passed or before it arrives. It thrives on imagination. Therefore fill your mind with peaceful thoughts so there's no room for anything else.

For Further Reflection
Isaiah 26:3

ENJOY TODAY

The future is today. Live for today, enjoy today—it comes but only once.

For Further Reflection
Psalm 118:24

SWAP BAD FOR GOOD

Suppression is not a good way to deal with bad feelings. Substitution is better. Rid yourself of them by transferring them with encouraging thoughts concerning God.

For Further Reflection
Ezekiel 18:31

SEEK PEACE

Follow after the things that make for peace …
things that are true, honest, and just.

For Further Reflection

Philippians 4:8
Romans 14:19

TURN SMILES INTO LAUGHTER

The ability to make someone laugh is a rare
creative gift, yet it only begins with a smile.

For Further Reflection

Psalm 126:2
Proverbs 15:13

EXPRESS YOURSELF

Writing out your troubled thoughts on paper
extracts the mind of haphazard thinking. Try
doing this and experience a mental release.

For Further Reflection

Jeremiah 30:2
1 John 1:4
Revelation 1:19

BE CREATIVE

"A picture paints a thousand words."
Try expressing yourself through painting
—it's a healing balm.

For Further Reflection

Philippians 4:7

BREATHE IN, BREATHE OUT

Deep rhythmic breathing is a splendid aid
to relaxation. It improves circulation, frees
the lungs, stimulates the brain, steadies the
nerves, and gives a feeling of control and
poise. Try it right now.

For Further Reflection

3 John 2

AFFIRM SOMEONE

Affirmations motivate us to move forward.
Try affirming someone today by giving
a genuine word of approval.

For Further Reflection

Philippians 2:3

BE CONTENT

Learn to be content with what you have:
a quiet home; a few books of inspiration;
a few trustworthy friends; and a hundred
innocent pleasures that bring no pain
or remorse.

For Further Reflection

1 Timothy 6:8

BE CHILDLIKE

Children have no thought for the past
or the future. They enjoy the moment.
Follow them into their beautiful and
enchanting world.

For Further Reflection

Matthew 19:14
Psalm 127:3

FIND SOLITUDE

Solitude is much more than the mere
absence of noise or cessation of movement.
In the midst of turmoil, you can have
stillness in the secret refuge of your soul.

For Further Reflection

Psalm 23
Psalm 72:3

GET A SOUL MATE

When you come across a kindred spirit who
sees you "eye to eye," regard the meeting
as having been brought by providence and
enjoy a new friendship. It was meant to be.

For Further Reflection

Proverbs 27:9

AVOID GLOOMY PEOPLE!

People who have gloomy moods attract to themselves gloomy people, and gloomy people have a knack of producing gloomy situations. Avoid them!

For Further Reflection

Proverbs 15:12, 18
Proverbs 22:24–25

LOOK FOR THE GOOD

When misfortunes arise, consider that it may be a blessing in disguise.

For Further Reflection

Deuteronomy 28:2
Ephesians 1:3

ANGEL DELIGHT

In times of need, remember that God sends his angels to camp around those who trust him, and to deliver them from their troubles.

For Further Reflection

Psalm 34:7

INSPIRE YOURSELF

In times of ailment very often the body will heal itself, especially when you feed the mind with words such as "Be strong and of a good courage."

For Further Reflection

Joshua 1:9

QUESTIONS, QUESTIONS

Serenity. Three phrases you should let go
from your mind if you want to be serene
are "what if only," and "why me?"

For Further Reflection

Proverbs 3:5–6

ACCEPT THE BEST

You can't have the best of everything,
but you can make the best of what
you've got.

For Further Reflection

1 Thessalonians 5:18

REACH FOR THE SKY

Your thoughts set the limits of your actions.
If you aim high you may not reach it,
but the spot at which you do arrive
may not be far off the mark.

For Further Reflection

Proverbs 23:7

MEDICINE FOR LIFE

Our rations of adversities are really medicines
prescribed by the Great Physician for our
ultimate benefit. Each dose contains
ingredients for eternal life.

For Further Reflection

Job 23:10

GET OVER IT!

No anxiety lasts forever or even for very long. Whatever you are going through, it, too, shall pass.

For Further Reflection

1 Peter 5:7

RESPECT YOURSELF, RESPECT OTHERS

"Do unto others as you would want them do to you." This is the golden rule of peace.

For Further Reflection

Luke 6:31

STAY CALM

Many aches and pains are of emotional origin. Back pain, excessive perspiration, palpitations, and ulcers: all have their root in negative emotion. Next time you feel discomfort, check your mood.

For Further Reflection

Psalm 25:18
Job 15:20
Daniel 5:6

APPRECIATE YOURSELF

Note the things you are good at and concentrate your efforts on them. Remind yourself from time to time of your worthwhile qualities. There's nothing wrong with self-praise.

For Further Reflection

Psalm 139:14

FIRST THINGS FIRST

The best anti-stress device is to start your
day with prayer and meditation.

For Further Reflection

Mark 1:35

KEEP YOUR FRIENDS

Take time off for friendship. Your quality of
life can be greatly enriched by maintaining
those special ties. So will theirs.

For Further Reflection

Proverbs 17:17

THE BEST MEDICINE

Laughter will lower your blood pressure, keep ulcers at bay, reduce your worries, tone up your nervous system, and above all make your face more pleasant to look at!

For Further Reflection

Proverbs 17:22
Proverbs 15:13

PRAY FOR DAILY BREAD

For each new day, pray for enough strength for that day, enough love for that day, enough hope for that day, enough peace for that day.

For Further Reflection

Psalm 29:11

KEEP YOUR MIND CLEAN

The human mind is the most powerful
healing force in the world, not matched
by any drug. Avoid contamination by
impure thoughts!

For Further Reflection

Jeremiah 4:14

HELP SOMEONE

However insignificant, try to make time
for one small act of service each day.

For Further Reflection

Ephesians 4:32

A HUG A DAY

Hugging is remedial. It ceases depression
and reduces stress. It has no unpleasant side
effects and is nothing less than a miracle
drug. Give someone a hug today!

For Further Reflection

Songs of Solomon 8:3

THINK POSITIVE

We can think of only one thought at any
given time. Invariably one kind of thought
is driven out by another. You can learn
to dispel negative thoughts by simply
replacing them with positive ones.

For Further Reflection

Philippians 2:6

SURRENDER

If you need reconciliation after a
disagreement with someone, try giving
a peace offering. It's a sure way of
starting a truce.

For Further Reflection

Proverbs 7:14

LOOK FOR THE GOOD

When misfortunes arise, consider that it
may be a blessing in disguise.

For Further Reflection

Deuteronomy 28:2
Ephesians 1:3

MEDITATE

"Whatsoever things are true, whatsoever things are lovely, and whatsoever things are honest, think on these things."

For Further Reflection
Philippians 4:8

WATCH OUT!

God has more for you! You haven't seen your best days yet. There's more ahead than behind you. So be prepared for exciting things.

For Further Reflection
Isaiah 43:18–19

CAST YOUR CARES

"Be anxious for nothing." All it does is
distort your mind.

For Further Reflection

1 Peter 5:7

SHOWERS OF BLESSING

To the stormy winds and waves Jesus said,
"Peace be still," and there was a great calm.
He can do the same in your storms of life.

For Further Reflection

Mark 4:39

BE MADE WHOLE

God's plan is not simply to repair your
brokenness; it is to make you a new creature.
That's why he's been revealing, removing,
and restoring certain things in your life.

For Further Reflection
2 Corinthians 5:17
Galatians 4:19

BE AN OVERCOMER

Jesus said: In this world you will have
tribulations, but be of good cheer, I have
overcome the world.

For Further Reflection
John 16:33

BE A PEACEMAKER

Blessed are the peacemakers, for they
shall be called God's children.

For Further Reflection

Matthew 5:9

IT'S GOD'S WAY, NOT YOURS

In difficult times, God teaches us that despite
our knowledge, skills, and experience to solve
problems, we only ultimately overcome "not
by might, nor by power, but by my spirit."

For Further Reflection

Zechariah 4:6

PEACE IN CRISIS

Guard your inward peace, even if your
whole world is in turmoil.

For Further Reflection

Psalm 112:6
Psalm 122:7–8

FREELY ACCEPT

Peace is one of the fruits of the Spirit.
It is the evidence of a spirit-filled life. The
good news is that God's Spirit is free to all.

For Further Reflection

Galatians 5:22

SELF-ANALYSIS
What's blocking you from experiencing
God's joy? Find out as soon as you can
and refuse to live another day with it.

For Further Reflection
Nehemiah 8:10

LIVE GOD'S WILL
When you know you're doing God's will,
you experience a lasting pleasure that
simply can't be found anywhere else!

For Further Reflection
Matthew 7:21

LOVE YOUR NEIGHBOR

Lets face it; sometimes confrontation does
end in permanent division. That's why "if
possible, live peaceably with all men."

For Further Reflection

Romans 12:18

LOOK FOR THE GOOD IN OTHERS

Compliments by their very nature are
biodegradable, and tend to dissolve hours
or days after we receive them; that is
why we can always use another.

For Further Reflection

Ephesians 4:25
Ephesians 6:8

BE AN INTERCESSOR

When God prompts you to pray for someone else, don't wait. Do it! Your prayers may be the only thing standing between that person and catastrophe.

For Further Reflection

2 Thessalonians 3:1

ADMIT YOUR FAULTS

One step toward recovering your peace is to admit that you are creating most of your stress.

For Further Reflection

Psalm 32:5
1 John 1:9

PRAY WITHOUT CEASING

Heaven stops to listen to your prayer.
Think about that! Your thoughts, struggles,
and goals may not mean much to others,
but they register with God.

For Further Reflection

1 Thessalonians 5:17

TURN STONES TO STEPS

Some people grow through failure, while
others never recover from it. What is the
difference? See your mistakes as stepping-
stones rather than stumbling blocks.

For Further Reflection

Psalm 130:4

READER'S
JOURNAL
for
Peace

Use the following pages to reflect on
the words you have read and any Bible
verses you have connected with.

_____

_____

_____

_____

_____

_____

_____

_____

_____

Hope

WORDS OF INSPIRATION
AND ENCOURAGEMENT

INTRODUCTION

In a time when things seem rather despairing and when the news of the day often seems to be nothing other than bad news, what hope is there? Today there are people dying with no hope and, perhaps even worse, people living without hope.

Yet such a seemingly dark and gloomy outlook is not the be all and end all: there is a ray of hope. We can experience life optimistically, expecting a bright future. It is God's desire that we live life abundantly.

I hope this chapter will provide some possible answers for life's worries, and enable you to experience a life worth living!

HOPE IN GOD'S PROMISES

We could never keep every promise we've
ever made. But God is 100 percent faithful.
Every one of God's promises is "yes" in Christ.

For Further Reflection

2 Corinthians 1:20

HOPE ON

Hope means hoping even when things
seem hopeless.

For Further Reflection

Joel 3:16

VALUE WHAT YOU HAVE

Never take a simple breath for granted.
It's a privilege to be alive. In spite of all
cruelty and unfairness, life is beautiful,
precious, and an incredible gift. Let us
make the best of it.

For Further Reflection

Psalm 8:3–6

NEW DAWN, NEW HOPE

Hope forever tells us that
tomorrow will be better.

For Further Reflection

Lamentations 3:22–23

WHEN ALL ELSE FAILS, TRY JESUS

If you have been reduced to God as your
only hope, you're in a good place.

For Further Reflection

Psalm 3:3
Psalm 39:7

BE HOPEFUL IN HOPELESSNESS

As long as matters seem hopeful, hope
remains merely superficial. It's only when
everything is hopeless, that hope truly
proves its strength.

For Further Reflection

Romans 8:24
Job 5:9

FIND HOPE WITHIN

"Life treasures are not far afield upon some distant shore. Jewels of peace and happiness are found right at your door."

Anonymous

For Further Reflection
Genesis 28:15

PERSEVERE

There are many lessons that can be learnt from watching children learn to walk. Countless times they fall, cry, and are hurt, but still get back up and try again. It's a sure reminder that what we want to accomplish may not always be easy. But persevere!

For Further Reflection
Matthew 24:13
Matthew 19:14

LET GOD LEAD

When the way forward seems a bit blurred, it can be God's way of getting you to recognize that things are changing. That's the time to consult him as to your next move.

For Further Reflection
Proverbs 3:5–6
Psalm 25:5

EXPLORE THE QUALITIES OF HOPE

Three relatives of hope:
Willingness—to accept whatever comes
knowing you'll come through stronger.
Determination—the ability to stand firm
while those around you are falling.
Insight—to see the character-developing
hand of God in it all.
With these qualities, you will survive!

For Further Reflection
Romans 5:3–4

DON'T SETTLE FOR SECOND BEST

Your biggest enemy is not the challenges you face; it's compliancy, negativity, self-imposed limitations, and self-pity. The Apostle Paul wrote "I can do all things through Christ who strengthens me." That means you can rise above circumstances, if you want to.

For Further Reflection
Philippians 4:13
Proverbs 13:12

BE AN ENCOURAGER

The world is full of discouragers—what we need is more encouragers. Many times a word of praise, thanks, or appreciation has kept a person on their feet. Encourage someone today: it will bring healing.

For Further Reflection
Proverbs 15:23
Isaiah 52:7

PRAYER CHANGES THINGS

When a believing person prays,
great things happen.

For Further Reflection

James 5:16

BE NOT DISMAYED

Remember, life will go on, even if it doesn't
go according to your plan. Don't wait until
you lose a loved one or have a heart attack
before you discover that. Your worth comes
from God, his opinion of you never changes.

For Further Reflection

Philippians 4:6

GIVE THANKS EVERY DAY

Finding time to pray every day will always
be a challenge, because prayer is a learnt
behavior. So, when you wake up, say,
"Lord, thank you for giving me this new day.
Help me to rejoice and be glad in it."

For Further Reflection
Psalm 100
Psalm 118:24

TAKE GOD AT HIS WORD

In life people will seek to offend you, for
whatever reason. What's important is not
what others say about you, it's what you
say to yourself. Affirm yourself by the
truth of God's word.

For Further Reflection
Psalm 139:16–18

LIVE TO YOUR POTENTIAL

You can never really tell what potential lies
within, until you have a purpose and a will
to achieve a goal. Life is an adventure;
we get out of it what we put into it.

For Further Reflection

John 10:10

LAUGHTER IS THE
BEST MEDICINE

It's a fact: laughter increases immunity, and
benefits cardiovascular, respiratory, digestive,
and muscular systems. It reduces pain and
stress, increases energy, and gives you a
sense of wellbeing. It's also contagious!

For Further Reflection

Proverbs 17:22
Ecclesiastes 3:4

BE PATIENT IN TRIBULATION

Happiness would not be fully appreciated
without an experience of its opposite,
sadness. Consider those who have
experienced such adversity and learn
from them.

For Further Reflection

Romans 12:12

THINK HAPPY THOUGHTS

Happiness is a product of attitude and
thought. It comes from you, not to you.
To be happy, you must think happy.

For Further Reflection

Psalm 128:2

LOOK FOR OPEN DOORS
When one door closes,
God always opens another.

For Further Reflection
Revelation 3:8

DISPEL YOUR FEARS
The one great enemy of the human race is
fear. The less fear you have, the more health
and harmony you will have. Remember fear
is a bluffer, it boasts more than it can really
do. Call its bluff, and it will disappear.

For Further Reflection
Isaiah 41:10–14

DON'T GIVE UP

One of the most common mistakes is thinking that success in life comes from some magical formula which we do not possess. Success is simply holding on and not letting go.

For Further Reflection
Revelation 3:11

DO SOMETHING CREATIVE

Develop a hobby. Do something for the sheer joy of it. Those who develop a creative and absorbing interest are better able to stand up to the stresses and strains of life.

For Further Reflection
Colossians 3:23

WORK THROUGH YOUR PROBLEMS

Don't run away from a problem, face it.
Chisel it into small parts, and deal with
each part separately.

For Further Reflection

Matthew 11:28–29
Psalm 55:22

REMINISCE TO REJUVENATE

What are your happiest moments? Savor
again an event of past years, or a long-ago
thrill, and some of the original warmth of the
occasion will return to cheer the present.

For Further Reflection

Deuteronomy 32:7
Proverbs 10:7

THERE'S POWER IN PRAYER

Why pray? Because nothing lies beyond the
reach of prayer. You'll never know how many
people have been strengthened because
you asked God to encourage them.

For Further Reflection

James 5:16

DEVELOP AN ATTITUDE
OF GRATITUDE

Though your present situation may seem
dismal, develop an attitude of gratitude.
It's surprising how just giving thanks in all
circumstances puts your life into perspective.

For Further Reflection

1 Thessalonians 5:18

THE BLESSED HOPE

The greatest hope you can ever have as a follower of Christ is the blessed hope of the glorious return of Jesus Christ our Lord.

For Further Reflection

Titus 3:6–7
John 14:1–3

SOUL FOOD

There is a common saying, "you are what you eat." In other words, to achieve good health we need a balanced diet. Likewise, reading the Bible gives spiritual food for our souls.

For Further Reflection

Deuteronomy 8:3

TRUST GOD'S TIMING

When God plants a dream in your heart,
he starts preparing you for its fulfilment.
He strengthens your character and deepens
your spiritual roots. Don't try to bring it to
birth prematurely, instead trust God's timing.

For Further Reflection
John 12:24

JUST FOR TODAY

This day will only come once. Challenge
yourself by saying, "Just for today I will enjoy
each moment to the fullest, and try not
to tackle all life's problems at once.
Just for today I will try to enjoy every
one of God's blessings."

For Further Reflection
Psalm 118:24

CONSIDER YOUR VALUE

Do you realize that when you put yourself
down, you're insulting your maker? God says
you are fearfully and wonderfully made:
in his eyes you are just right.

For Further Reflection

Psalm 139:14
Ephesians 1:11

TRUST GOD

There is only one person who is ultimately
faithful, reliable, and dependable and in whom
we can fully trust. As the Scriptures declare,
"Put not your hope in man in whom there
is no hope, but put your hope in God."

For Further Reflection

Psalm 146:3
Lamentations 3:24

HOLD ON

When it seems that your prayers are not
being answered, it may be that God is simply
saying "hold on." During this time he will
be healing your past so it cannot pollute
your future.

For Further Reflection

Isaiah 49:8

NOTHING IS TOO HARD FOR GOD

Nothing shocks God, or catches him off
guard. When the crisis you're facing makes
you want to throw in the towel, remember
your problems are his opportunities.

For Further Reflection

Matthew 19:26
Mark 14:36

LET IT GO

The word "forgive" literally means "to give away": it has very little to do with the other person; it's a decision you make, like exhaling carbon dioxide from your body because you know holding on to it will only harm you. So go ahead, exhale: release forgiveness.

For Further Reflection

Matthew 6:12–15

START TODAY

The first step to pursuing joy is simply to begin. The Psalmist says, "This is the day that the Lord has made; let us rejoice and be glad in it." If we wait until conditions are perfect, it will never happen.

For Further Reflection

Psalm 118:24
Psalm 68:3

HOW PRECIOUS YOU ARE

The fact that God cares for you may be hard
to hold on to when you are having a bad day;
but to be cared for means to be wanted, and
despite your failures, God still wants you. It's a
truth that will never go away, so accept it!

For Further Reflection
John 15:15

LEARN TO RELAX

Hope fades when we constantly get uptight
about everything: being five minutes
late, getting stuck in traffic, waiting in
line, overcooking a meal, gaining weight,
discovering another gray hair. Lighten up—
release the tension and let hope soar.

For Further Reflection
Romans 5:5
Ecclesiastes 3:12–13

GET STAYING POWER

In times of powerlessness it's comforting
to know that God gives power to the weak,
and to those who have no might,
he increases strength.

For Further Reflection

Isaiah 40:29
Isaiah 61:1

MORE HOPE, LESS WORRY

The Bible says, "The Lord is faithful, he will
guard you from evil." You may not know what
you're being protected from, but God knows:
he saves your life every day! So trust him
more, complain less; hope in him more,
and worry less.

For Further Reflection

2 Thessalonians 3:3
Psalm 103:4

CAPTURE NEGATIVE THOUGHTS

Low self-esteem arises when we listen to lies about ourselves. When a negative thought enters your mind that could be crippling to your character, capture it, assess it, measure it up to what God thinks of you, and if it doesn't match up, throw it out!

For Further Reflection

2 Corinthians 10:5
Philippians 4:7

PUT YOUR FAITH TO THE TEST

When you are overwhelmed, it is easy to jump to the conclusion that God isn't on the job. When you can't figure it out, you have to faith it out!

For Further Reflection

Psalm 9:10–11

USE WHAT YOU'VE GOT

It's easy to use our limitations as an excuse
for doing nothing productive with our lives.
But God wants you to develop your strengths
and fulfil your life's purpose. So instead
of dwelling on what you don't have, start
using what you have.

For Further Reflection

Ephesians 2:10

TAKE GOD AT HIS WORD

God has given us his "promise and his oath,"
so in prayer, even though you may not get
the answer you want, you can rest assured he
makes "everything work together for good."

For Further Reflection

Hebrews 6:18
Romans 8:28

APPRECIATE YOURSELF

Everything God made was very good; that
means you, too. Endeavor to see yourself
as God sees you: he wants to change
your self-image so you can appreciate
your unique gifts and qualities.

For Further Reflection
Genesis 1:31

CHERISH WHAT'S YOURS

Learning to be content with what we have
puts what we hope for in perspective.
The last commandment says "do not covet."
Once we're satisfied with what we've got,
our hopes will not be covetous.

For Further Reflection
Philippians 4:11
1 Timothy 6:8

ENJOY THE MOMENT

When you appreciate the moment, you instinctively know that as long as you have life, you have hope. Enjoy the moment.

For Further Reflection

Deuteronomy 4:4
Luke 19:9

CHOOSE TO BE HAPPY

Happiness is not something you pursue; indeed the more you pursue it, the more elusive it becomes. Happiness is something you can choose to accept right now.

For Further Reflection

Psalm 128:2
Acts 26:2

BE OPTIMISTIC ABOUT LIFE

One of the discoveries of modern medicine
is that the more optimistic you are, the
greater your chances of maintaining health.
Simply believe that you will be well:
you've got nothing to lose.

For Further Reflection

Isaiah 65:18
Luke 6:23
James 5:13

PUT HOPE INTO ACTION

Some conclude that hope is merely an expectation of certain
outcomes. It's more than this: hope is a real commitment to
positive behavior and attitudes. It's an active, positive
word. Adapt this approach and live an abundant life.

For Further Reflection

Romans 15:13
Romans 12:12

BE CALM

A calm state of mind is naturally
accompanied by hope and optimism.
Maintain the calm, and you maintain
the hope.

For Further Reflection

John 14:27
Romans 15:13

GET EXCITED ABOUT SOMETHING

Enthusiasm. What a wonderful action word!
It is an effective, contagious force. It helps
you achieve the impossible and makes the
future full of promise. Be enthusiastic!

For Further Reflection

Psalm 32:11
Psalm 47:1

GIVE, AND IT WILL COME BACK TO YOU

When you go out of your way to do good for others you derive a double benefit. First, any selfless act generates a feeling of wellbeing, and second, your outlook on life becomes more meaningful.

For Further Reflection

Luke 6:38
2 Corinthians 9:6–8

CELEBRATE LIFE

Your birthday is a wonderful opportunity to celebrate the miraculous achievement of what your life has been to date. If there's one thing that's worth celebrating, it's the fact that you are alive.

For Further Reflection

Luke 12:23
John 10:10

MAKE UP YOUR MIND

Abraham Lincoln said, "A man is as happy
as he makes up his mind to be." The same
can be said of hope: you're as hopeful as
you make up your mind to be.

For Further Reflection

Psalm 45:2
Psalm 71:5,14

GO BACK TO THE FUTURE

Generally, the problems of today become
less threatening with the course of time.
If you imagine yourself at some time in the
future looking back on your worries today,
you'll discover they were not worth
worrying about at all.

For Further Reflection

Matthew 6:25–34

BE THE CHANGE

Gandhi once said, "Be the change you want
to see in the world." There's no better place
to begin than with yourself.

For Further Reflection

Psalm 51:10

TREASURE YOUR TREASURED
MOMENTS

When you have an inspiring thought or
experience, keep a journal to treasure these
moments. Over a period of time you will
build a collection of your own personal
inspirations to refer to in times of need.

For Further Reflection

Isaiah 30:8
Jeremiah 30:2
Revelation 1:19

KEEP ON KEEPING ON

There is one trait that produces more
positive results than knowledge, wealth,
or fame—persistence. If you just keep
going, maintaining your hope and belief
that something good will happen,
eventually it will.

For Further Reflection

2 Timothy 4:5

CHANGE YOUR WAYS

It's never too late to change bad habits,
unhelpful patterns of behavior, fixed
routines, or mundane cycles. All it takes is
commitment, and a change of perspective,
and you can alter the negative.

For Further Reflection

Philippians 3:21

LOOK FORWARD WITH HOPE

No matter how dark and dreary the days
ahead may seem, there is always something
positive to look forward to that can become
your beam of light. Just flick on the switch.

For Further Reflection

Hebrews 12:2

DON'T STAY DOWN

Life is all about learning from our mistakes;
and the beauty of it is that no matter how
many times we fail, there's always another
chance. Failure is not the falling down;
it's the staying down.

For Further Reflection

Psalm 37:24

DON'T BE MISERABLE

Miserable people get the same number
of opportunities as happy people. They just
tend to overlook them. Look for the good
and you'll feel much more hopeful.

For Further Reflection

Isaiah 45:22

KEEP FIT, FEEL GOOD

As we know, exercise brings our body to
an overall state of good health. It also has
benefits spiritually. By giving us a vitality for
life, exercise gives us a more hopeful outlook.
Isn't that worth working up a sweat for?

For Further Reflection

3 John 2

TURN TO THE SUN

Let the rays of the sun permeate your soul.
Sunlight, apart from being a good source
of vitamin D, staves off those melancholy
moments, and injects hopefulness and
vibrancy into your day.

For Further Reflection

Matthew 13:43

YOU ARE WHAT YOU THINK

The words you use, like your thoughts, have
a powerful influence on how you behave.
Reinforce your positive behavior by telling
yourself, "there is much to live for,"
"life does get better," "there is hope."

For Further Reflection

Proverbs 23:78

YOU ARE INDISPENSABLE

Remember, you are unique. There is no one
else on this planet like you. You are one of a
kind, just as important as anyone else in this
world, and the contribution you make is vital.
So take your rightful place on the podium.

For Further Reflection

Isaiah 43:2

SOW A LITTLE HOPE

The growth cycle of a plant reassures us
of the continuity of life. Germination, the
sprouting plant, its growth, and its eventual
natural recycling, all show us that there
is order and purpose in life.

For Further Reflection

Psalm 126:6

ENDURE YOUR TEST

What may seem to you to be bitter trials are often blessings in disguise. Take comfort in the hope that when you come through, you will be stronger, as gold tried in the fire.

For Further Reflection
1 Peter 1:7

RELAX YOUR FACE AND SMILE

Smiling relaxes your face. You use less facial muscles than when frowning and communicate good feelings toward others and within yourself.

For Further Reflection
Proverbs 15:13
Nehemiah 2:2

KEEP FOCUSED

When you have a purpose in life, you will
be less affected by the obstacles that get
in your way. Instead of seeing them as
hindrances, they become stepping
stones to success.

For Further Reflection

Philippians 3:13–14

RELEASE YOUR POTENTIAL

Every new opportunity in life remains only
potential until you take that first step forward.
Go forward, take the first step, and the rest
of the journey will take care of itself.

For Further Reflection

Psalm 16:11
Psalm 119:105

THE SERENITY OF PRAYER

"God grant me the courage to change
the things I can, the patience to accept
the things I can't, and the wisdom to
know the difference."

Reinhold Niebuhr

For Further Reflection

James 1:5

IT GETS EASIER

It's always the beginning of a task that
seems the most challenging—riding a bike,
playing the piano, learning a language. It's
most difficult just before it starts to get easier.
So take courage: when it seems daunting,
your life could be about to turn for the better.

For Further Reflection

2 Timothy 2:3
Matthew 24:13

WAR OF THE MIND

You can think yourself into happiness or
success, despair, or hopefulness. It all depends
how you manage the volume of one type
of thought over the other. The one that
dominates the mind tends to be the winner.
The good thing is that you decide
who will win.

For Further Reflection

Isaiah 26:3
Luke 12:29

LOOK UP

It's only when we walk with our head down
that we bump into lamp posts—with our
chin up and head straight, in the dark the
same lamp post becomes our light and guide.

For Further Reflection

Micah 7:7

IT'S WORTH THE WAIT

On earth we have the pain without the reason. In heaven we have the reason without the pain.

For Further Reflection
Revelation 21:4

GO FORWARD

There are many things in life that we have no control over, especially things in the past. Acknowledging these areas in life will enable us to move forward and create new pathways for the future.

For Further Reflection
Isaiah 38:17
Philippians 3:13

DON'T WORRY

The things we worry about rarely become a reality. It's like dynamite without a flame to light it, potentially destructive but actually powerless. In fact, the only damage it does is rob you of a hopeful tomorrow.

For Further Reflection

Philippians 4:6

THINK AHEAD

You limit your future when you dwell in the past. You can accomplish a lot more by envisioning your future plans. Actualize it in your mind, see it before it happens.

For Further Reflection

Proverbs 23:4

TREAT OTHERS WELL

"Do unto others as you would have them
do unto you." The golden rule, if practiced, can lead
to a golden experience and hopeful outlook.

For Further Reflection

Micah 12:33
Leviticus 19:18

TAKE NOTHING FOR GRANTED

When you lower your assumptions of what
you expect from other people, you will
receive a welcome surprise. Assume nothing,
but know that great things lie ahead for you.

For Further Reflection

Philippians 2:3

LESSONS FROM A BABY

The birth of a baby is the personification of hope. It ought to remind you not only of a perfect creator, but also a perfect sustainer of life.

For Further Reflection

Ecclesiastes 9:4
Romans 8:24

CHOOSE A POSITIVE RING TONE

Choose a ring tone that instils positive thoughts every time it rings. Not only will you not mind the phone ringing, but the words will reinforce feelings of wellbeing. How about "I Feel Good" by James Brown!

For Further Reflection

2 Chronicles 7:6
1 Samuel 16:23

LOOK FOR THE GOOD

Despite our faults or failings, we all have
something positive that's worthwhile.
To discover it in those around you, just
look for it—but be aware, it may mean
choosing to ignore the negative.

For Further Reflection
Proverbs 12:25,15:23
1 Thessalonians 5:21

SHOW GENUINE LOVE

Amid so many rules and laws, we're told to
abide by two commands: "Love your God
with all your heart," and "Love your fellow
men." If we truly practice this, everything
else will fall into place.

For Further Reflection
Mark 12:28–33

ACT WHAT YOU BELIEVE

When you act as though life has something special in store for you, you'll soon discover it's true. Not only is it a biblical promise, but you also convince your subconscious, and this becomes self-fulfilling.

For Further Reflection

Mark 9:23

"BIG UP" YOURSELF

If no one else is around to compliment you, go ahead and do it yourself. Congratulate and reassure yourself. If there's one person it pays to have on your side, it's you!

For Further Reflection

Psalm 139:14

MAINTAIN YOUR FRIENDSHIPS

An important factor in inspiring you to be hopeful is the support of old friends. Treasure those associations—it's so easy to be "out of sight, out of mind." If you have an old friend, don't let them go.

For Further Reflection
Proverbs 17:17

DON'T NEGLECT GOD'S LEADING

Sometimes we forget the struggles we've been through and how God helped us get through them. Take time out today and reflect on how God has helped you in the past. It will give you added confidence for the future.

For Further Reflection
Isaiah 46:9

ALL THINGS BRIGHT AND BEAUTIFUL

If you want to inject feelings of brightness
and jubilance, surround yourself with
colorful flowers. The fragrance alone
acts as a healing balm.

For Further Reflection

Isaiah 40:6

MAINTAIN YOUR INTEGRITY

The satisfaction of a job well done will bring
rewards of its own. If you work diligently and
faithfully, you not only feel a greater sense of
achievement, but contentment that you've
done your best, even if no one else notices.

For Further Reflection

Proverbs 13:11

READ MORE, WATCH LESS

Usually your imagination is more active
when you're reading than when you're
watching. That's why literature can have a
more uplifting and long-lasting effect than
more passive mediums of entertainment.
Spend time reading books, and let your
imagination work.

For Further Reflection
2 Timothy 2:15

A PRAYER OF HOPE

Thank you Lord for filling my past and my
present with your love, your mercy, and your
grace. Thank you for the promise that I can
spend all my tomorrows with you.

For Further Reflection
Hebrews 6:19

A POEM OF HOPE

"Be content, my heart, though you cannot
see God's vast eternal mystery. Be at peace,
my soul, like a child at rest, in the simple
truth that God knows best."

Anonymous

For Further Reflection

2 Corinthians 4:16–18

A TIME TO DANCE

The wise king Solomon said, "for everything
there is a season," and goes on to list
many events in life. When you've cried all
your tears, dance. You'll be surprised
how therapeutic it can be.

For Further Reflection

2 Samuel 6:14
Psalm 30:11

HOPE IN GOD

Remember, God is not bound by our circumstances, neither is he overcome by our turmoil. In every situation he has power to provide a way out for you. Put your hope in him.

For Further Reflection
Psalm 121:1–3

THE HOPE OF THE WORLD

"Life with Christ is an endless hope, without him a hopeless end."

Anonymous

For Further Reflection
Philippians 1:20–21

LOOK UP

When looking backward is filled with pain
and looking forward seems ominous;
try looking upward.

For Further Reflection

Psalm 107:28–30

HOLD ON TO HOPE

"Today well-lived makes every tomorrow
a vision of hope."

Anonymous

For Further Reflection

Romans 15:13

HOPE IN THE FUTURE

As a believer in God you can confidently say,
"Although I don't know what the future holds,
I know who holds the future!"

For Further Reflection

Deuteronomy 1:29–30

BE PROACTIVE

Don't wait for the opportunities to do good,
make the opportunities.

For Further Reflection

Colossians 1:10
Proverbs 12:25

YOU'RE NEVER ALONE

When you're alone, you can be certain of
one thing: even though you may not feel his
presence, God is with you—he will never
fail in his promises.

For Further Reflection

Joshua 1:5–6

A BEACON OF HOPE

"The world cries out with a common voice,
'Is there hope? Where can hope be?' To our
wounded world God still replies, 'With the
cross of Calvary.'"

B.J. Huff

For Further Reflection

Isaiah 55:3

DECIDE ON YOUR OWN ENDING

Do not think of your problems as a full stop,
but merely as a comma. You can decide how
the rest of the sentence will run.

For Further Reflection

Philippians 1:6

LET HOPE HEAL

In times of illness, the human body
experiences a natural gravitational pull in the
direction of hope. That's why the patient's
hope is the physician's secret weapon. It is
the hidden ingredient in any prescription.

For Further Reflection

Jeremiah 17:143

CAST YOUR CARES ON HIM

At the cross, Jesus took on all our sins and
troubles and placed them on himself. Yet the
sacrifice wasn't just a one-off, he is more than
willing to do it for you again and again.
What sacrificial love!

For Further Reflection

Romans 5:8

FEAR NOT

The fear of what might happen tomorrow
is far worse than the actual experience
of any present sorrow. Don't take upon
yourself unnecessary pain. Ask God
to banish the fears.

For Further Reflection

Lamentations 3:57–58

FOCUS ON THE LITTLE THINGS

It is the little things that usually have the greatest impact in life—a compliment, a smile, a thank you, a hug. It's these things that make up a positive outlook.

For Further Reflection
Luke 19:17

NEVER GIVE IN

"Never give in, never give in. Never, never, never, never—in nothing, great or small, large or petty, never give in, except to convictions of honor and good sense."

Winston Churchill

For Further Reflection
Jeremiah 7:24
1 Thessalonians 5:21

START AFRESH

"Today is the first day of the rest of your life."

Dale Carnegie

For Further Reflection

Proverbs 4:18
Psalm 118:24

HOPE IS LIFE

"What oxygen is to the lungs, such is hope
to the meaning of life."

Emil Brunner

For Further Reflection

1 Timothy 4:9–10

ACT ON INSPIRATION

It's not inspiring books or presentations that change people's lives; they simply act as a catalyst. It is what you choose to believe and act upon, that's where the change comes. No one can change the life of any individual except that individual.

For Further Reflection

Joshua 24:15

CLAIM THE GIFT

"Yesterday's history,
Tomorrow's a mystery.
All we have is Today, and it's
called the present
Because it's a precious gift."

Anonymous

For Further Reflection

James 1:17

METAMORPHOSIS

What the caterpillar sees as the end,
the butterfly sees as just the beginning.
It's the same life with a new outfit.

For Further Reflection
2 Corinthians 5:17

YOU ARE WHO YOU ARE

When you start comparing yourself with
others, eventually you will become either
resentful or vain, for there will always be
greater or lesser people than you. Be yourself.
Accept yourself. Appreciate yourself!

For Further Reflection
1 Peter 2:9

ATTITUDE PROBLEMS

Your attitude dictates your whole approach
to life. The good news is, you can alter your
life simply by changing your attitude.

For Further Reflection

Psalm 37:5

TRUST YOURSELF

Intuition is the ability to discern based on
instinct. To many questions of your life, the
answers really lie within. Instead of constantly
listening to others—listen to yourself.
You are your own solution.

For Further Reflection

Isaiah 30:21

GET UP AGAIN

Falling down is a temporary condition.
Staying down is what makes it permanent.

For Further Reflection

Isaiah 37:24
Micah 7:8

DON'T LET GO

"When you get to the end of the rope,
tie a knot and hold on."

Franklin D. Roosevelt

For Further Reflection

1 Thessalonians 5:21

FLEE TEMPTATION

We are promised that in every tempting
situation, there is always a way of escape.
Don't get caught, look for the exit.

For Further Reflection

1 Corinthians 10:13
Revelation 3:100

HERE TODAY, GONE TOMORROW

"And it came to pass," is a common phrase
in the Old Testament. It is a reminder that,
whatever our present turmoil—be hopeful,
it too will pass.

For Further Reflection

2 Samuel 11:1–2
Romans 8:18

BELIEVE, AND YOU WILL

If you believe you can, you can.
If you believe you can't, you can't.
So what do you want to believe?

For Further Reflection

Mark 11:24
Mark 9:23

LEAVE IT TO GOD

"If we have faith the size of a mustard seed,
we can move mountains." Don't look at the
mountain, look to the mountain mover.

For Further Reflection

Matthew 17:20
Matthew 21:21

DAILY PRAYER

"Lord, let me live one day at a time.
My choice determined by your will,
My path illumined by light,
My faith grounded in your truth,
My heart set on eternity."

For Further Reflection

Proverbs 4:11

EXPECT THE UNEXPECTED

If you travel a path in life without obstacles,
you're probably going around in circles.
The only guaranteed thing in life is its
unexpectedness.

For Further Reflection

John 16:33

DO IT EVEN WHEN AFRAID

Facing our fears is sometimes the hardest
thing to do. Not everything that is faced
can be changed, but nothing can be
changed unless it is faced.

For Further Reflection

Isaiah 41:10
Exodus 14:13

TRY NOTHING, GAIN NOTHING

What would you attempt to do if you knew
you would fail? What would you lose
if you never attempted? In every attempt
there's always a lesson.

For Further Reflection

1 Samuel 17:32
Luke 22:33

COUNT YOUR BLESSINGS

The words of the hymn writer still ring true, "Count your blessings, name them one by one … and it will surprise you what the Lord has done." That's one hymn worth putting into practice!

For Further Reflection

Ephesians 1:3
Malachi 3:10

LEARN YOUR LESSONS

When you've come through your test in life, commune with God to discover what lesson he would have you learn.

For Further Reflection

Psalm 25:4

LOOK ON THE BRIGHT SIDE

Find courage in dis-courage-ment.
An appointment in dis-appointments
and hope in hope-lessness.

For Further Reflection

Job 41:22
Psalm 30:11

BE PATIENT

Whether it's the best of times or the
worst of times, remember there are
other times to come.

For Further Reflection

Psalm 30:5

LOOK TO THE CROSS

We all have our crosses to bear, some large, some small, but because of the cross Christ carried, we all have the hope of eternal life.

For Further Reflection
1 John 2:25

TURN IT OVER TO JESUS

We are invited to "cast our burdens on the Lord," with the promise, "he will sustain you." The emphasis is on "sustain"—that means to strengthen and nourish you throughout.

For Further Reflection
Psalm 55:22
1 Peter 5:7

KEEP GOING

If you're going through hell—
don't stop, keep going!

For Further Reflection

Isaiah 43:2
Matthew 24:13

WAIT FOR THE MORNING

The Psalmist provides this wonderful verse:
"Weeping may endure for the night, but joy
comes in the morning."

For Further Reflection

Psalm 30:5

HEAD FOR THE STARS

"Two men looked out of prison bars,
one saw mud, the other saw stars."

Dale Carnegie

For Further Reflection
Deuteronomy 4:19
Psalm 121:1

YOU HAVE AN INVISIBLE FRIEND

Unseen by us, within the spiritual realm
at any time needed, God sends his angels
of hope to bring us invincible help.
You are not alone.

For Further Reflection
Psalm 91:11
Psalm 34:7

FOOTPRINTS IN THE SAND

When you think your prayers are not being answered and you see only one set of footprints in the sand, be assured they're not yours—God is carrying you, and your load.

For Further Reflection

Isaiah 53:4

GOD IS OMNIPRESENT

Since Jesus Christ is "the same yesterday, today and forever," we can take the Christ of yesterday; walk with him today, and ask him to guide our paths for tomorrow— for he's already there.

For Further Reflection

Hebrews 13:8
Psalm 139:7

GOD HAS A PLAN FOR YOU

"For I know the thoughts I think towards you," says the Lord, "thoughts of peace and not of evil, to give you a future and a hope."

For Further Reflection
Jeremiah 29:11

LEAN ON GOD

To put your faith in God is to lean your whole weight upon him. It also means removing the crutch.

For Further Reflection
Proverbs 3:4–5

GOOD THINGS COME TO THOSE WHO WAIT

"Those who wait on the Lord shall renew their strength; they shall mount up with wings like eagles. They shall run and not be weary, they shall walk and not faint."

For Further Reflection

Isaiah 40:37

LET GOD WORK IT OUT

Leaving the details of your future in God's hands is the most responsible act of obedience you can make. It's also the ultimate act of faith.

For Further Reflection

Romans 8:28

BE SPIRIT-LED

"Trust in the Lord with all your heart and
lean not on your own understanding;
in all your ways acknowledge him and
he shall direct your paths."

For Further Reflection
Proverbs 3:5–6

AVOID A QUICK FIX

When we present our problems to God
he doesn't give temporary relief,
he offers a permanent solution.

For Further Reflection
2 Thessalonians 2:16
Isaiah 26:4
Isaiah 60:19–20

SAVED BY GRACE

"Amazing grace, how sweet the sound
that saved a wretch like me,
I once was lost but now am found
Was blind but now I see."

John Newton

For Further Reflection
Ephesians 2:5,8

HOPE CHANGES THE WORLD

"Everything that is done in the world
is done by hope."

Martin Luther

For Further Reflection
Ecclesiastes 9:4
Romans 8:24

CHERISH YOUR EXPERIENCES

Experience comes by persevering through
life's encounters. It is a valuable asset. Every
addition to it enhances your life.

For Further Reflection

James 1:2

LOOK TO THE LIGHT

No one ever damaged their eyesight
by looking on the brighter side of life.

For Further Reflection

2 Corinthians 4:18
Isaiah 45:22

SUBMIT TO GOD

When we fully surrender to Christ, we begin
to look at life through his eyes, and we learn
to face the future through his strength.

For Further Reflection

James 4:7

BE A COMFORTER

When God comforts us it's not necessarily
to make us comfortable, but, once comforted,
to then go on and be a comforter to others.

For Further Reflection

2 Corinthians 1:3–5

GOD MOLD YOU

As the potter is to the clay, so God is to our lives. However you might presently feel, remember, God has not finished with you yet.

For Further Reflection

Jeremiah 18:6

EXPERIENCE A NEW LIFE

Conversion is a wonderful spiritual term. It means rebirth—a new life. It is the ultimate source of hope for the person who wants a change in their life.

For Further Reflection

Luke 22:32
John 3:6

READER'S
JOURNAL
for
Hope

Use the following pages to reflect on
the words you have read and any Bible
verses you have connected with.

Joy

WORDS TO CHEER
AND DELIGHT

INTRODUCTION

Unlike other emotions, joy is a constant
state of wellbeing that does not change with
the surrounding circumstances of life that
often influence our feelings. Joy is an inner
confidence, knowing that God is there and
there is nothing to fear for the future. It is also
an acknowledgment of being the recipient
of the present blessings from him.

This chapter is designed to help you to be
in tune with this source of joy, and to challenge
you to step out in faith that you will begin
to see the fruits of living a life free from
the cares and worries of this world.

CLAIM YOUR JOY

It is God's every desire that your
life be filled with joy. To you he says,
"May your joy be full."

For Further Reflection
John 15:11

BELIEVE IN YOURSELF

Look in the mirror. Go ahead, face
yourself and announce, "I'm full of
untapped potential."

For Further Reflection
Philippians 2:13

GET INFECTED

"Joy is very infectious … be always
full of joy."

Mother Teresa

For Further Reflection
Matthew 10:8

JOY FOR KEEPS

When God gives you joy,
no one can take it from you.

For Further Reflection
John 16:22

FINISH YOUR TO DO LIST

Set reasonable goals so that by the
end of the week you can complete your
tasks. When Friday comes, feel the
weight of worry lift off your shoulders.

For Further Reflection
Genesis 2:1–2

SHOUT TO THE LORD

Whether or not you can sing,
you can "make a joyful noise unto
the Lord."

For Further Reflection
Psalm 100

OPEN THE DOOR

God knows how to turn things around.
He can turn your sorrow into
joy—just let him in.

For Further Reflection
Psalm 41:22
Jeremiah 31:13

RENEW YOUR JOY DAILY

The reason God blesses you
every day is simply because he wants
you to be joyful every day.

For Further Reflection
Ecclesiastes 7:14

A STEADFAST JOY

To be joyful is a principle. It doesn't change
with emotions. Joy is an inner contentment
despite all the circumstances.

For Further Reflection

Ecclesiastes 2:10
Ezra 6:22

GET POWER THROUGH JOY

The scriptures declare, "the joy
of the Lord is your strength."

For Further Reflection

Nehemiah 8:10

WAIT FOR THE HARVEST
"They that sow in tears
shall reap in joy."

For Further Reflection
Psalm 126:5

SEEK GOD'S WILL
Make sure that what you want is
what God wants for you! Then your
joy will be complete.

For Further Reflection
Ephesians 5:16–17

RISE ABOVE YOURSELF

Mediocrity is just the best of
the worst and the worst of the best.
Is that what you want? No? Then
get out of your comfort zone!

For Further Reflection

Ecclesiastes 9:10

LET GOD FIX IT

If God's dealing with greed, lust, pride,
or any other obstacle in your path—
don't get in his way!

For Further Reflection

John 3:6

LET GOD FINISH

To be joyful … try less and trust more. The
Bible says, "he who began a good work
in you will carry it on to completion."

For Further Reflection
Philippians 1:6

BE GRATEFUL

When you consider that God knows
all about your sin, yet promises to
offer forgiveness, it ought to give
you a heart of thankfulness.

For Further Reflection
Daniel 9:10

FORGIVE JOYFULLY

Real forgiveness is a lifelong
commitment. You must practice it
every day. It's not easy, but the rewards
abound in joy.

For Further Reflection
2 Corinthians 2:7
Luke 6:37

MAKE THE RIGHT CHOICE

"You can think and act yourself into
dullness or unhappiness. By the same
process you can build up inspiration
and a surging depth of joy."

Norman Vincent Peale

For Further Reflection
Deuteronomy 30:19–20

EMBRACE GOD'S LOVE

God's love will heal your emotions,
raise your self-esteem, and put a
foundation of self-worth and joy within
you. Embrace that love today.

For Further Reflection
Romans 8:31–39

REST UP

Your joy can easily be robbed when
you allow yourself to become emotionally
and physically drained. Reclaim your
joy by seeking tranquillity.

For Further Reflection
Isaiah 30:15

ORDER YOUR PRIORITIES

To live a life with joy is more rewarding
than a "successful" life without it.

For Further Reflection

Job 20:5

LOOK FOR JOYFUL SIGNS

You will know when you are joyful
in the Lord; it leads to the feelings of
praise, thankfulness, worship, and
adoration of God.

For Further Reflection

Psalm 34:1

TASTE THE FRUITS

The fruits of the Spirit are love, joy,
peace, patience, kindness, goodness,
faithfulness, humility, and self-control.

For Further Reflection

Galatians 5:22

SERVE JOYFULLY

Acts of service always lead
to scenes of joy.

For Further Reflection

1 Corinthians 13:4

THE WORD OF LIFE

The words in the Bible contain so much life and power. They're stronger than any therapy. God can give you a word that goes back into your past, and heal your yesterday, secure your today, and anchor your tomorrow. Start tapping into that power today.

For Further Reflection
Ephesians 3:20

APPRECIATE GOOD IN OTHERS

It takes more than one color to make a rainbow. When you learn to appreciate the difference in people, you will find it all contributes to the whole picture.

For Further Reflection
Philippians 2:2–3

DO IT 100 PERCENT
Be absolutely determined to
enjoy what you do.

For Further Reflection
1 Corinthians 10:31

GIVE YOURSELF BACK TO GOD
Consider your life as a gift
from the Creator. Your gift back
is letting him fill it with joy.

For Further Reflection
Luke 6:38

PASS JOY ON
To have joy is to share it.

For Further Reflection
2 Corinthians 9:7
Acts 20:35

WORK, REST, AND PLAY
Live and work but don't forget to
play, have fun in life, and really
enjoy it.

For Further Reflection
Philippians 2:2

SAFEGUARD YOUR JOY
Don't let anyone steal your joy!

For Further Reflection
Revelation 3:11

SEEK JOY FROM GOD
Remember, joy never came from riches
or wealth or the praise of men. Such a
belief will always be a myth.

For Further Reflection
Acts 8:20
1 Timothy 6:10

BE A BLESSING

Since you get more joy out of giving
to others, put a lot more thought
and effort into the happiness you
are able to give.

For Further Reflection

Romans 12:14

CULTIVATE JOY

"The greater part of our joy or misery
depends on our dispositions and not on
our circumstances. We carry the seeds of one
or the other in our minds wherever we go."

Martha Washington

For Further Reflection

Psalm 126:6

DON'T SETTLE
FOR HALF MEASURES

Jesus said, "These things have I spoken
to you that my joy might remain in
you and that your joy might be full."

For Further Reflection
John 15:11–12

SACRIFICIAL GIVING

"There is a wonderful law of nature that
the three things we crave most in life—
joy, freedom, and peace of mind—
are always attained by giving them
to someone else."

Peyton Conway March

For Further Reflection
Matthew 25:35–40

ENJOY YOURSELF!

It's a misconception to believe that having fun can't be God's will. The God who made giraffes, a puppy's tail and a young girl's giggle has a sense of humor. Make no mistake about that!

For Further Reflection

Psalm 37:4

THE TIME IS NOW

If you are unable to experience joy in this season of your life, what other season shall you wait for?

For Further Reflection

2 Kings 7:9

CHOOSE LASTING JOY

The difference between shallow happiness
and a deep joy is sorrow. When sorrow
arrives, happiness, dies. It can't stand pain.
Joy, on the other hand, rises from sorrow
and therefore withstands all grief.

For Further Reflection

Job 41:22
Psalm 51:11

TRUST IN GOD

Joy is the deep-seated confidence
that God is in control of every
area of your life.

For Further Reflection

Proverbs 3:5–6

STOP COMPLAINING

"The happiest people don't worry
too much about whether life is fair
or not, they just get on with it."

Andrew Matthews

For Further Reflection

Proverbs 16:20
John 6:43
Philippians 2:14

FIND JOY THROUGH TRIALS

The things we try to avoid and
fight against—tribulation, suffering, and
persecution—are the very things that
produce abundant joy in us.

For Further Reflection

Romans 8:37
2 Corinthians 7:4

TRUST GOD'S TIMING

"Our Heavenly Father never takes anything from his children unless he means to give them something better."

George Müller

For Further Reflection
Luke 11:10–13

FOLLOW CHRIST'S EXAMPLE

The joy Jesus experienced came from doing what his Father sent him to do. He says to us, "As the Father sent me, so send I you."

For Further Reflection
John 20:21

BE TRANSFORMED

"God not only takes away the
bitterness in your life and gives
sweetness in its place, but turns the
bitterness into something itself."

Charles Spurgeon

For Further Reflection
Jeremiah 13:13

EXPERIENCE HEALING JOY

The experience of joy has many
healing wonders; it strengthens your
immune system, burns away impurities,
shapes your intellect, and disperses worries
and other negative emotions.

For Further Reflection
Isaiah 35:102–3

LIFT HIM UP!
"Rejoice in the Lord always;
again I say rejoice."

For Further Reflection
Philippians 4:4

BE CHILDLIKE
Children smile 400 times a day on average …
adults 15 times. Children laugh 150 times
a day … adults 6 times. Children play
4–6 hours a day … adults only 20 minutes.
What has happened?

For Further Reflection
Ecclesiastes 12:1–7

THE JOY IN YOU

Joy has nothing to do with material
things. A person living in luxury can
be wretched, yet a person in the depths
of poverty, overflowing with joy.
Joy's not in things, it's in you!

For Further Reflection

Proverbs 23:7
Luke 6:45

GET INTO PERSPECTIVE

"In the end it's not the years in
your life that count. It's the life
in your years."

Abraham Lincoln

For Further Reflection
John 10:10

THE FUTURE'S BRIGHT

"A pessimist sees the difficulty in
every opportunity; an optimist sees the
opportunity in every difficulty."

Winston Churchill

For Further Reflection
Psalm 71:14
Lamentations 3:26

EVERY DAY IS A GIFT

"The greatest gift you can receive,
is another day of life."

Anonymous

For Further Reflection
James 1:17
2 Kings 7:9

JOYFUL IN SADNESS

We can be joyful and happy at the
same time, but more importantly, when
life's circumstances deal us a hard blow
we can be joyful though unhappy.

For Further Reflection

Psalm 35:9
2 Corinthians 7:4

REVEL IN SIMPLICITY

Buy a single rose, tulip, or daisy. Admire
the smell, color, and shape of the petals and
remember how beautiful life can be.

For Further Reflection

Genesis 1:31
Psalm 104:24

JUMP FOR JOY

Literally. Hopping up and down
for 30 seconds infuses you with
energy and youthful vigor.

For Further Reflection
John 3:2

MEDITATE WHILE YOU WALK

Stroll through a familiar part of town
and focus your mind on sights,
smells, and sounds.

For Further Reflection
Psalm 8:3

REMEMBER KIND ACTS

Recall a situation in which a friend
treated you kindly. Mentally extend
the feelings of joy that inspired you.

For Further Reflection

2 Peter 1:7–8

DO THE TWIST

This dance style is fun, silly, and easy
and it will make you laugh.

For Further Reflection

Psalm 30:11
Ecclesiastes 3:4

CREATE AMBIANCE

For tonight's dinner, put out your best
tablecloth, create a centerpiece, or simply
light a candle. A festive setting makes
for a festive mood.

For Further Reflection
2 Timothy 6:17

GET OUTSIDE

Joy is the deep-seated confidence
that God is in control of every
area of your life.

For Further Reflection
Psalm 121:1

TAKE LESSONS

It's not too late to learn a hobby ... like
knitting, playing the piano, horse riding ...
hobbies are fun and release stress.

For Further Reflection

Ecclesiastes 2:10

LOOK TO THE HEAVENS

Whenever possible, relax under
the stars. Gazing at the night sky makes
you feel more connected to the world.

For Further Reflection

Job 22:12
Romans 1:21

STAY CONNECTED

Jesus says, "I am the vine, you are the branches." You are not blessed in any endeavor because of your performance, you're blessed because of your connection to the vine.

For Further Reflection
John 15:5

FORGIVE IT AND DROP IT

You cannot really forgive without the Holy Spirit's help. None of us can. So today why don't you pray, "Holy Spirit, breathe on me and give me the strength to forgive _____ for what they did. Heal me of my wounds …"

For Further Reflection
Mark 11:25

INTERCEDE

Prayer isn't just about you. It's about others.
Your prayer moves God. God moves people.
People bring about change. The whole thing
begins with one praying person—today
let that person be you.

For Further Reflection

Psalm 106:23

A JOY THAT TRANSFORMS

If you're tired of the way your life's
going and don't like what you're becoming,
pray the Psalmist David's prayer in Psalm 51:
"Create in me a clean heart and renew
in me a right spirit."

For Further Reflection

Psalm 51

ACCEPT GOD'S WORD

God's promises NEVER FAIL … Every one
of them are like precious jewels just
waiting to be discovered.

For Further Reflection

2 Peter 3:9
2 Corinthians 1:20

CLAIM GOD'S PROMISES

Because your God is a covenant-making,
covenant-keeping God, what he has spoken
over your life he will surely bring to pass.
Depend on it. God keeps his word.

For Further Reflection

Romans 3:4

BE JOYFUL IN PATIENCE

No matter how long it takes, wait
for God's timing. He always shows
up at the right time.

For Further Reflection

Isaiah 40:31
Lamentations 3:26

LET GO OF HATRED

Endeavor to forgive those who
have done you wrong, just as Christ
has forgiven you. Bitterness is fatal.
It kills your joy.

For Further Reflection

Colossians 3:13

CONFESS AND FORSAKE

"Confession is good for the soul." It cleanses
and purges you from guilt and shame
and allows the Spirit of Jesus to surface
once again.

For Further Reflection

Proverbs 28:13
1 John 1:9

DETERMINE YOUR PRIORITIES

If you're too busy to reach out
to those who are hurting, you're
just too busy!

For Further Reflection

Luke 10:33

START AFRESH TODAY

You can't do anything about your past,
but starting right now you can change
your future—one choice and one
act at a time.

For Further Reflection
Matthew 16:27

HEAVENWARD BOUND

Many of the rewards God has for
you are so great it'll take eternity to
appreciate and enjoy them. That's why
he wants you in heaven!

For Further Reflection
Luke 14:14
John 14:1–3

JUDGE NOT

When God wants to bless you, sometimes
he'll send a person—your boss, the tax man,
the mortgage lender, the postman, or even
those who mean you no good!

For Further Reflection

Philippians 4:19

TRUST GOD'S FAITHFULNESS

When you appreciate God's blessings you
will be able to say in difficult times, "If he
blessed me before, he'll do it again"—
and press on.

For Further Reflection

Hebrews 13:8
Malachi 3:6

STEP UP

When God is on your side, obstacles
become opportunities for growth!

For Further Reflection

Philippians 3:13–14

LET GO

Waiting is difficult but it serves a
vital purpose. Above all else it means
making a daily decision to trust and obey
God even when things are not going
the way you planned.

For Further Reflection

Hebrews 6:15

GET CLEAN

When you accept Christ, he changes
you from the inside out.

For Further Reflection
2 Corinthians 5:17

IN HEAVEN'S EYES

Through prayer you get to know God's
heart and start seeing yourself through
his eyes. When that happens you'll never
see yourself in the same way again!

For Further Reflection
Isaiah 55:8
1 Corinthians 13:12

DON'T LOSE HEART

Regardless of your circumstances,
keep your joy alive today by staying
focused on God!

For Further Reflection

Job 11:18

SEE THE GOOD

Being joyful is letting those we love
be perfectly themselves, not twisting them
to fit our own image. Otherwise our joy
will only be based on the reflection of
ourselves that we see in them.

For Further Reflection

Colossians 3:13

BE AMAZED BY GRACE

No matter what you've done or how
far you've fallen, you can receive
God's love and joy and mercy.
It's called grace.

For Further Reflection

Ephesians 2:5
2 Corinthians 12:9

AN AWESOME GOD

Jesus is the only man ever to make an
appointment beyond the grave and show up
for it! That's the kind of God you serve!

For Further Reflection

John 11:25

KEEP THE COMMANDMENTS

When asked to identify what the
law was about, Christ simply replied,
"Love God and love people." This is
the foundation of joy.

For Further Reflection

1 John 4:8

CHECK YOUR ATTITUDE

Mother Teresa always worked with a joyful
attitude. If somebody could be joyful
amongst the dying and the poorest of
the poor, surely you can too!

For Further Reflection

Isaiah 61:10

KEEP ON PRAISING

To maintain a joyful attitude the
Psalmist said, "seven times a day
I praise you"—try it.

For Further Reflection
Psalm 119:164

GET YOURSELF RECYCLED

Christ loves to salvage and recycle the
hurting, the throw-aways, the left-overs,
the used-ups and the put-downs,
and fill them with joy.

For Further Reflection
Luke 19:10

LEAD BY EXAMPLE

Your Bible knowledge may be 10 times
greater than someone else's, but if you're
not 10 times more loving, patient,
and joyful, what good is it?

For Further Reflection

Deuteronomy 11:18

TIME FOR A SCRUB

God's word is the only detergent strong
enough to get down into the deepest
levels of our thoughts, imagination, and
motives and cleanse us.

For Further Reflection

Hebrews 4:12

PASS IT ON
You're blessed to be a blessing.

For Further Reflection
Genesis 12:2

OPEN THE DOOR
"If you want joy, real joy, wonderful joy ... let Jesus come into your heart."

Joseph D. Carlson

For Further Reflection
Proverbs 23:26
Revelation 3:20

THE REASON FOR THE SEASON

"Joy to the world. The Lord has come."
This favorite carol reflects the true
reason why we can have joy today.

For Further Reflection

Matthew 1:21

LIVE TO GIVE

There is tremendous joy in giving.
It is a very important part of
the joy of living.

For Further Reflection

Matthew 10:8

DON'T WASTE TIME

Time is fleeting. Often a second
chance never comes. Don't hesitate
to do something good—a note
of appreciation, a card of thanks,
a word of gratitude.

For Further Reflection
John 9:4
Matthew 25:13
Proverbs 27:1

A NEW HOPE

Today is a new day ... a fresh start.

For Further Reflection
Lamentations 3:23

BE PROACTIVE

Refuse to spend time worrying about
what might happen. Determine to spend
time making things happen.

For Further Reflection
1 Corinthians 3:14
2 Thessalonians 1:11

LET JOY RADIATE FROM YOU

Joyful people are more likely to be
confident, positive in thinking, healthy,
and have attractive personalities.
It certainly pays off!

For Further Reflection
Proverbs 15:13

WATCH OUT FOR COMPLACENCY

Constantly thank God for the things
we often take for granted … sight, sound,
touch, taste, hearing … and loved ones!

For Further Reflection

Songs of Solomon 8:7

THE BEST MEDICINE

Laughter is "to express emotion or
amusement by expelling air from the
lungs in short bursts to produce an
inarticulate voiced noise." All you need
is something to trigger it off!

For Further Reflection

Ecclesiastes 3:4

KEEP JOY ALIVE

If joy is strength, its absence
creates weakness.

For Further Reflection

Nehemiah 8:10

JUST DO IT

If we wait until conditions are perfect,
it will never happen. If we are going to
rejoice, find a reason today.

For Further Reflection

Psalm 68:3
Psalm 118:24

CAST YOUR BURDENS

Worry makes us depend on ourselves,
it robs us of joy and energy.

For Further Reflection
Proverbs 24:19

CHOSEN

With full knowledge of your
past failings and present defects
of character, God chose you anyway.
That is mind-blowing grace!

For Further Reflection
John 15:16

CHECK YOUR MOTIVES

If you feel unrecognized and
unrewarded for what you do, ask
yourself: "who am I doing it for?"

For Further Reflection

1 Corinthians 10:31

NURTURE JOY

While God has given us the
capacity for joy, we must make every
effort to develop that joy, release it,
and walk in it at all times.

For Further Reflection

2 Timothy 1:6

PUT OTHERS FIRST
Only when we decide to
practice sacrificial love and put away
the old "me-first" lifestyle, will the joy
and power of God's love be released
through our lives.

For Further Reflection
Ephesians 5:2

REFLECT YOUR JOY
The most readily identifiable
outward characteristic of the Christian
is joy. If something has happened inside,
it ought to show on the outside!

For Further Reflection
Matthew 5:16

NEGATIVE TO POSITIVE
The Psalmist said "It was good
for me to be afflicted so that I might
learn your decrees." God loves to turn
our negatives into positives.

For Further Reflection
Psalm 119:71

FIND JOY WITHIN
"Joy is not in things, it is in us."

Richard Wagner

For Further Reflection
Isaiah 30:29
Matthew 5:8

THANKS FOR EVERYTHING

Paul writes "In everything give thanks …"
In uncertainty give thanks, in heartache
give thanks. In poverty and in
prosperity give thanks.

For Further Reflection

1 Thessalonians 5:18

BE IN CONTROL

When you can laugh in spite of your
circumstances, it shows that temporal
situations don't control your joy.

For Further Reflection

Proverbs 17:22

BE AN ENCOURAGER

We all need encouragement and
the beautiful thing about encouraging
is that anybody can do it.

For Further Reflection
1 Thessalonians 5:11

STICK AT IT

Jesus said, "You will weep and
mourn … but eventually your grief
will turn to joy … and no one
will take it away."

For Further Reflection
Luke 16:20–22

BE DIVINELY PROTECTED

If we saw the snares Satan
lays for us … how we would adore
the Lord who enables us to
escape them all!

For Further Reflection
Psalm 103:2

A NEW LEASE OF LIFE

The Psalmist said, "The Lord … redeems
your life from destruction." When others
write you off, he signs you up.

For Further Reflection
Psalm 103:2

BE YOUR OWN AUTHOR

Your life is a story. Each day you get
to write a new page. So, fill those pages
with joyful moments. When you look
back you won't be disappointed.

For Further Reflection
2 Timothy 4:7

SPEND PRECIOUS MOMENTS

Spend quality time with those people
in your life to whom you're irreplaceable.

For Further Reflection
Psalm 90:12

DON'T WASTE TIME

Time is an equal-opportunity employer.
We all get 24 hours / 1,440 minutes / 86,400
seconds daily and we must account for
how we use them.

For Further Reflection
Romans 14:2

LET JOY FLOW

When you bless others, you open
up your heart as a channel for God
to bless you.

For Further Reflection
Acts 20:35
Ephesians 6:8

BE SATISFIED

Be careful for the love of "more."
You risk losing appreciation of your
God-given blessings.

For Further Reflection

Hebrews 13:5

SEEK CONTENTMENT

The Apostle Paul says, "I have learned
in whatever state I am, to be content."
That's something to strive for!

For Further Reflection

Philippians 4:11
Proverbs 15:16

JUST BE SATISFIED

Pursue the virtue of contentment,
for "Godliness with contentment
is great gain."

For Further Reflection
1 Timothy 6:6

LET GOD RESHAPE YOU

God doesn't waste anything. He uses
all our experiences—the good, the bad,
and the ugly—to prepare us.

For Further Reflection
Philippians 3:21

WAIT FOR THE REASON

If you're struggling to see God's purpose in your suffering today, rest assured he has one. When you trust him, he makes "all things work together for good."

For Further Reflection

Romans 8:28

LOVE GOD, LOVE OTHERS

Contentment and fulfilment are achieved when we walk straight along the path the Lord has set before us.

For Further Reflection

Psalm 119:105
Matthew 19:17

EXPERIENCE JOY IN DOING

"Do all the good you can, by all the means
you can, in all the places you can at all the
times you can to all the people you can,
as long as you ever can."

John Wesley

For Further Reflection
Zechariah 4:10

STAYING POWER

God doesn't just strengthen you once …
He'll strengthen you again and again
as and when the need arises.

For Further Reflection
Ephesians 6:13

JOYOUS IN WAITING

Just because it hasn't happened yet
doesn't mean God has changed his mind.
While you are waiting, God is working.

For Further Reflection

James 1:4

JOYFULLY ASSURED

"You can start thanking God today
for what he will do for you tomorrow,
because he will, absolutely will,
come through for you!"

Richard Wagner

For Further Reflection

Isaiah 65:24

BE JOYFUL IN PRAYER
Our goal in prayer should be to
maintain such a close relationship with God
that we can communicate back and forth
no matter what the time of day or situation.

For Further Reflection
Ephesians 3:12

WORRY KILLS JOY
If we really believe that God cares
for us—we won't need to worry
about worrying things.

For Further Reflection
Psalm 23:4
Matthew 8:26

TAKE IT OR LEAVE IT

Joy is not something that comes in
different levels, portions, or sizes—you
either have it, or you don't.

For Further Reflection
John 16:24

BE AN OPEN CHANNEL

Like the Dead Sea, God never intended
us to be reservoirs that just take in.
He called us to be rivers that flow
out to bless others.

For Further Reflection
Proverbs 11:24–25
2 Corinthians 9:7–8
Ecclesiastes 11:1–2

SOW JOYFUL SEEDS

Even if you don't have a specific
need right now, sow a seed of kindness ...
you never know who might reap it
in the future.

For Further Reflection

Psalm 126:5
Hosea 10:12

LOVE IN ACTION

Loving God is an attitude resulting
in action. It's a daily decision to
acknowledge him in all that you
say and do.

For Further Reflection

Revelation 2:4
1 Corinthians 13:7–8

BEING LOVED LEADS TO JOY

Sometimes our actions make us
unlovely but we are never unloved.
Because God loves us we are valued.
Enjoy that thought.

For Further Reflection

1 John 3:1

PLANS TO PROSPER YOU

How do you know if God still
has a plan for you? Because you are
still breathing! His plans never expire.

For Further Reflection

Jeremiah 29:11

PRACTICE WHAT YOU PREACH

How much of the advice you give to
others do you actually practice yourself?
Living what you believe to be true is a
sure path to joyful living.

For Further Reflection

Mark 4:14
Colossians 3:17
James 1:22

DON'T LOSE YOUR TEMPER

Next time you get all worked up ask
yourself, "What is the enemy trying to do
here?" Be sure, ultimately he wants
to steal your joy?

For Further Reflection

Ephesians 4:27

LOVE YOURSELF AGAIN

Times of despondency, despair, and
depression can often remove feelings of
self-worth and love. It's during the
time of darkness that God's light seeks
to shine brighter, reminding you that
you are precious.

For Further Reflection

Psalm 139:17
Jeremiah 31:3

HAPPY ARE THE JOYFUL

Joy is more than what we call happiness.
Joy is the enjoyment of God and the
good things that come from him.

For Further Reflection

Psalm 16:11
Romans 14:17

FILL UP CONTINUALLY
Joy is the fuel God injects in our life for it to run on.

For Further Reflection
Romans 15:13

NEW DAY, NEW BEGINNINGS
Welcome each new morning with a
smile on your face, love in your heart,
and good thoughts on your mind.

For Further Reflection
Psalm 63:5
Isaiah 61:10

CHERISH THE GIFT

This day with its blessings and
challenges is a gift from God, so don't
insult him by complaining.

For Further Reflection

Philippians 2:14

GROW OLD GRACIOUSLY

A life of gratitude and service will
keep you young until you die. A life of
complaining will age you prematurely.
Stop your complaining!

For Further Reflection

Ephesians 5:20
1 Timothy 4:3
Psalm 26:7

TAKE CONTROL

"To get up each morning with the
resolve to be happy ... is to set our
own conditions to the events of the day.
To do this is to condition circumstances
instead of being controlled by them."

Ralph Emerson

For Further Reflection
1 Corinthians 1:17–18

OBEY THE COMMANDER

"Rejoice in the Lord always!"
Joy is a command. It's non-optional
and non-negotiable.

For Further Reflection
Deuteronomy 28:8
Psalm 42:8

BOUGHT WITH A PRICE

Just think: the God of the universe
willingly left the splendor of heaven, was
born into poverty and died for wayward
humanity. Why? That we may have
abundant joy in him!

For Further Reflection

Philippians 2:7

BE SHAPED BY THE POTTER

You may be "flawed" and "limited" but
the God who lives and works in you is not!

For Further Reflection

Philippians 2:13

DISCOVER YOUR GIFTS

Often the qualities we see in other
people are already available within you.
Cultivate your God-given gifts
and appreciate them.

For Further Reflection

2 Corinthians 4:7

THE BLESSED HOPE

In order to keep us from becoming
too attached to this world, God reminds
us of its ugliness—to keep our hearts
longing for a better world.

For Further Reflection

John 14:1–3
1 Peter 1:17

PERSONALIZE YOUR JOY

Repeat this sentence by filling in
the blank with your name:
God loves _____ so much that he
died so that _____ can experience
God's joy in his / her life today!

For Further Reflection

Mark 9:23
John 1:7
John 11:40

SMALL GIFTS

Life's most rewarding experiences
rarely come in neat little packages.
They're often found in little unexpected
encounters. Watch out for them!

For Further Reflection

Luke 10:31–32

JUST ASK

If you want joy in your life
then sincerely ask God for it. It's that
simple! He's waiting to bestow it
within you today!

For Further Reflection

Matthew 7:7–8

READER'S
JOURNAL
for
Joy

Use the following pages to reflect on
the words you have read and any Bible
verses you have connected with.